ARENA EVENTS
PRO WRESTLING

KENNY ABOO

Fly!
An Imprint of Abdo Zoom
abdobooks.com

abdobooks.com

Published by Abdo Zoom, a division of ABDO, P.O. Box 398166, Minneapolis, Minnesota 55439. Copyright © 2019 by Abdo Consulting Group, Inc. International copyrights reserved in all countries. No part of this book may be reproduced in any form without written permission from the publisher. Fly!™ is a trademark and logo of Abdo Zoom.

Printed in the United States of America, North Mankato, Minnesota.
092018
012019

THIS BOOK CONTAINS RECYCLED MATERIALS

Photo Credits: Alamy, AP Images, Getty Images, Icon Sportswire, Shutterstock
Production Contributors: Kenny Abdo, Jennie Forsberg, Grace Hansen
Design Contributors: Dorothy Toth, Neil Klinepier

Library of Congress Control Number: 2018946210

Publisher's Cataloging-in-Publication Data

Names: Abdo, Kenny, author.
Title: Pro Wrestling / by Kenny Abdo.
Description: Minneapolis, Minnesota : Abdo Zoom, 2019 | Series: Arena events |
    Includes online resources and index.
Identifiers: ISBN 9781532125379 (lib. bdg.) | ISBN 9781641856843 (pbk.) |
    ISBN 9781532126390 (ebook) | ISBN 9781532126901 (Read-to-me ebook)
Subjects: LCSH: WrestleMania--Juvenile literature. | Wrestling matches--Juvenile
    literature. | World Wrestling Entertainment, Inc.--Juvenile literature.
Classification: DDC 796.8120--dc23

TABLE OF CONTENTS

PRO WRESTLING

From the top ropes, pro wrestling has **dominated** fans for more than 60 years!

At each match, the greatest wrestlers come together to battle for the chance to show who is the best in the **ring**.

OPENING ACT

In 1952, the Capitol Wrestling Corporation (CWC) was created to **promote** boxing and wrestling. It was renamed the World Wrestling Foundation (WWF) in 1979.

9

Many famous wrestlers joined in the 1980s making it a huge television hit. Two wrestling specials aired on MTV. *The Brawl to End It All* and *The War to Settle the Score* were held in 1984 and 1985 respectively. Each of the **title** winners would go on to the main event.

11

WrestleMania was born on March 31, 1985, at Madison Square Garden in New York City. The main event was Hulk Hogan and Mr. T teaming up against Roddy Piper and Paul Orndorff.

Fans loved it so much, that it became a yearly event. The WWF changed its name to World Wrestling Entertainment (WWE) in 2002.

THE MAIN EVENT

The longest WrestleMania match lasted more than one hour. It was between Bret Hart and Shawn Michaels at WrestleMania 12. The shortest was between The Rock and Erick Rowan during WrestleMania 32. It lasted just six seconds.

The event that broke **attendance** records was Collision in Korea in 1995. More than 170,000 hard-core fans packed the May Day Stadium in Pyongyang, North Korea.

19

WWE is one of the world's most valuable sporting companies in the world. In 2018, it raked in more than $280 million!

GLOSSARY

attendance – the number of people at an event.

dominate – being the best person or thing in something.

promotion (wrestling) – a company that puts on regular shows. WWE, TNA, and New Japan Pro Wrestling are examples of promotions.

ring – a space surrounded by an audience in which a sport takes place.

title – the position of being the best in a major event.

ONLINE RESOURCES

Booklinks
NONFICTION NETWORK
FREE! ONLINE NONFICTION RESOURCES

To learn more about pro wrestling, please visit abdobooklinks.com. These links are routinely monitored and updated to provide the most current information available.

INDEX